QUEST FOR WORLD
DOMINATION

STEPHAN A. DZEROVYCH

authorHOUSE

AuthorHouse™
1663 Liberty Drive
Bloomington, IN 47403
www.authorhouse.com
Phone: 833-262-8899

Published by AuthorHouse 05/11/2021

ISBN: 978-1-6655-2470-4 (sc)
ISBN: 978-1-6655-2471-1 (hc)
ISBN: 978-1-6655-2474-2 (e)

Library of Congress Control Number: 2021908877

CONTENTS

FOREWORD

Relationships between nations are no different than those between people.

People with common interests tend to become good friends. Nations with similar policies and strategies become allies. People treated poorly by others become enemies. Nations that sustain adversary actions from other nations become enemies. Some people strive all their lives to become rich and influential. Others are content with a comfortable life. Some nations persevere to become superpowers. Other nations have modest goals.

ASCENT OF US TO WORLD SUPERPOWER

With the dissolution of the Soviet Union on December 26, 1991, the United States clearly became the only superpower in the world. Its economy was by far the largest in the world and on the international scene the US had enormous influence on world affairs. The US military strength and technological capabilities had no equal. As the nominal head of NATO, the US controlled a powerful and expanding military establishment consisting at that time of 16 member nations. Through its Western allies the US had close ties to the European Union (EU) and maintained major military bases in the UK, Germany, Italy, Belgium, Spain, Portugal and Iceland.

The US military power was fully demonstrated during the Gulf War in 1991, when an US assembled multi-national coalition was able to oust Saddam Hussein's invading Iraqi forces from Kuwait in less than two months to the acclaim of the world. The victory over Hussein gave the United States confidence that it can count on international cooperation when it comes to promoting justice and democracy around the world.

The US global policy at that time became strictly dictated by national security interests, the most fundamental of which was to create a secure, prosperous and democratic world for the American people. Having triumphed over Communism, the United States was confident it could export its vision of liberal democracy, in which individual rights and freedom under the rule of law are protected, to the rest of the world. It also became firmly convinced that an opportunity opened up to reconstruct the world's geopolitical scene, and establish a new, more favorable world order which it could control for decades to come.

A typical course of action would involve support to governments to promote democratic reforms, provide economic assistance and set up a security agreement, which could include installation of military bases. When confronting dictatorial governments, political pressure would be exerted on the authoritarian regimes to comply with accepted democratic principles and human rights standards. Furthermore, sanctions would be applied when international obligations are violated. If it was determined that a regime change is in order, support to internal or external opposition groups would be provided to isolate or weaken the regime and thus facilitate the transition. With regard to economy, emphasis would be placed on the need to adhere to free market principles, giving US companies the opportunity to invest in world's industries and thus gain a measure of economic leverage. By promoting globalization, the national economy would be integrated through trade, investment and capital flow on the international scale.

This concept of a new world order was first pronounced during the George H.W. Bush administration in the 1990 to 1991 period and was subsequently endorsed by future administrations. The policy also received full backing from conservative US lawmakers, elder statesmen, corporate elite, and the military industrial complex who are known to constitute a kind of guardian shadow government, often referred to as the "Deep State" in the political arena.

The US policy of spreading liberal democracy around the world started in the Middle East and included maintaining a permanent US naval presence in the Persian Gulf to preserve peace in the region. The policy had a negative response from the Moslem world, viewing it as a revival of the Christian Crusades.

The Middle East at the turn of the 20th century was a powder keg ready to explode. In Iraq, Saddam Hussein, a Sunni Moslem dictator who was just defeated by a US led coalition in the Gulf War, was firmly subjugating an underprivileged majority Shiite population. In Syria, an

Alawite regime under President Assad was firmly ruling a deprived and impoverished Sunni majority population. The continued presence of US troops in Saudi Arabia was an instant irritant to Moslems because the Saudi kingdom houses some of the holiest sites in Islam. The peace process between Israel and the Palistinian Authority was stalled, as the main issues, the status of Jerusalem, final borders, fate of Israeli settlements and destiny of Palistinian refugees, could not be resolved. Overall, there was a growing inherent animosity among the Moslem populations toward the West for its political and economic exploitation as well as its imposition of Western ideas by advocating liberal democracy and globalization, as they contradicted their social customs and religious beliefs. They rejected the imposition of these idealogies as tools of colonialism.

Most of the Islamic states of the Middle East were also considerably underdeveloped compared to the modern West and rapidly modernizing Orient. The majority of the Moslem countries of the region were economically depressed with high unemployment rates among its largely restless young populations. A high degree of corruption predominated the governing elite. These conditions led to the development of a breeding ground for terrorists.

The main terrorist threat against the United States at that time came from al-Qaeda, a Moslem terrorist group headed by Osama bin Laden. The group had weapon facilities in several Middle East countries and training facilities in Afghanistan. Al-Qaeda's principal aim was to inspire and incite Islamist movements and the Moslem masses worldwide to attack those perceived to be enemies of Islam including the United States. The group was able to gain sympathy among the Moslem masses by exploiting the widespread suffering, resentment and anger in the Moslem world, and turning it against the US and its allies.

After several terrorist attacks on US facilities in the Middle East and Africa, on September 11, 2001, hijackers belonging to the al-Qaeda organization crashed two airplanes into the World Trade Center in New York City and into the

Pentagon. A total of 2977 people were killed and more than 6000 others injured.

Realizing that Osama bin Laden was behind the 9/11 plot, the United States gave the Taliban government of Afghanistan one final chance to turn him over to the US. They declined and the United States invaded Afghanistan on October 7, 2001. Almost ten years later, Osama bin Laden was killed by US Navy Seals in Pakistan on May 1, 2011.

The 9/11 terrorist attack was a major setback for the United States because of the realization that despite counting a number of Middle East countries as their allies, the threat from Moslem extremists and terrorists among them was real and needed to be addressed urgently to make US safe.

The prevailing opinion of the United States administration was that a new, more aggressive Middle East policy was needed to protect US interests in the region and counter the increasing threat from Moslem terrorists and Islamic countries considered hostile to the US.

In the State of the Union address on January 29, 2002, President George Bush laid out a near term road map for the US. This road map identified the key actions that needed to be taken to secure a safe world for the United States.

Iraq, Iran and North Korea were singled out for persuing weapons of mass destruction and deemed an "axis of evil". Without stating it directly, the primary US policy became to seek a change in the governments of these countries through any means necessary, including resort to force. The intention was to bring to power regimes that would be friendly to the United States and its interests, endorse democracy and serve the purpose of supporting the ultimate national objective of a more secure world under US oversight. Control over Iraq and Iran would assure an uninterrupted flow of oil to the West, critical at that time to the industries of the United States and its Western allies. Furthermore, it would open the gates to further advances to the East including Afghanistan, Russia and eventually China. Although Russia remained subdued after losing the

Cold War and China was still in the build-up process, both of these countries were considered in the long term to be the main threats to US dominance of the world. Gaining a position of influence in both Iraq and Iran would isolate Russia from the South and provide a pathway of allied countries leading toward China's borders. Control over North Korea would eliminate its long range nuclear threat to the US and its Asian allies as well as put political and military pressure on China.

To avoid the perception of an unilateral political and military undertaking by the United States, it became imperative under the doctrine to enlist the support of at least some of the West European and Asian allies to underscore that the nation-building activity was a multi-nation coalition effort.

Considering the geopolitical advantages, the primary geographic area to be addressed under the new policy became the Middle East, the central part of an Islamic Belt stretching from the northwest tip of Africa into Asia. The governments of this region consisted mostly of autocratic Moslem governments and monarchies not universally friendly to the United States and hostile towards Israel, an important US ally.

EVIL ONE - IRAQ

The next major action under the new doctrine came against Saddam Hussein's Iraq, one of the countries singled out by President Bush in 2002 as a member of the axis of evil. On the pretext that Iraq was harboring weapons of mass destruction, Operation Iraq Freedom was launched on March 20, 2003, by a combined US and British force. The operation lacked UN support and approval. Saddam Hussein's regime collapsed in several weeks and the war was officially declared over on May 1, 2003. Saddam Hussein was captured on December 13 of the same year and executed on December 30, 2006. However, no evidence of weapons of mass destruction was ever found. The misjudgement was later attributed by US to faulty intelligence.

Despite the overthrow of Hussein and the installation of a new Iraqi government, an unexpectedly strong insurgence continued. As law and order broke down, sectarian tensions and score settling between Shiite and Sunni Moslem Iraqis grew. The US and its coalition partners responded with force to the growing insurgency, which only alienated the Iraqi population. It became difficult to convince the Iraqi people of the benefits that peace and democracy would bring, when you carry a gun and they have a copy of the Koran in their back pocket that tells them differently.

As tensions between Shiites and Sunnis accelerated, Sunni terrorist groups, particularly al-Qaeda in Iraq and later Islamic State of Iraq (ISI), became prominent and sought to expel US forces from Iraq. The US position was made difficult by the religious shism of the Sunni and Shiite religions, as it became problematic to build trust and alliances. An alliance with one religious group immediately turned the group of the other religion against you.

In 2009, after a new Iraqi government under Prime Minister Nouri al-Maliki attained some measure of control, the United States started a phased withdrawal of its forces from Iraq. After all the US forces withdrew from Iraq, the Iraqi Armed Forces assumed all security responsibilities. However, the terrorist groups never came under full control and over time their threat only increased. Consequently, the main thrust of the US military engagement in Iraq to establish a peaceful order in this part of the Middle East favorable to its national interests was not successful. On the contrary, the undertaking led to an unsettled environment in all of the Middle East which set the stage for the region's explosion in violance that eventually involved most of the countries of the region, and which persists until today.

EMERGENCE OF
ISIS - IRAQ AND SYRIA CONFLICTS

In late 2010, a series of anti-government rebellions called the Arab Spring spread across the Middle East, resulting eventually in change of governments in Tunisia, Libya, Egypt and Yemen. However, only the uprising in Tunisia resulted in a transition to a constitutional government, prompting the disappointed and oppressed Arab masses to further violence.

In Syria, the Arab Spring inspired the Sunni majority to protest against the Alawite regime of President Assad. Their calling for Assad's removal escalated to a civil war when the regime tried to violently suppress them. In Iraq, an Islamic terrorist military force was organized by Abu Bakr al-Baghdadi by recruiting former Iraqi military and intelligence service officers who had served under Saddam Hussein. The group grew in size and force as Moslems with Islamic convictions from countries around the world started to join it, and funds as well as weapons from Moslem countries friendly to their cause began to be clandestinely supplied to it. Eventually, the terrorist group was able to control about half of Iraq's territory and to infiltrate into Syria in the midst of a raging civil war.

On June 29, 2014, after occupying the eastern part of Syria, it proclaimed itself to be the Islamic State of Iraq and Syria (ISIS) and the worldwide Caliphate, making Baghdadi the self-declared authority over the world's 1.7 billion Moslems.

In addition to ISIS there were other Islamic terrorist factions, most notably al-Nusra Front (also designated as al-Qaeda in Syria) and the Free Syrian Army (FSA), whose goal was also to bring down the government of Bashar al-Assad of Syria. Al-Qaeda in Syria, an affiliate of the terrorist organization responsible for the 9/11 attack, was firmly opposed by the United States and all Western coalition countries. The Free Syrian Army, however, even though at times it acted in concert with ISIS and al-Qaeda in its battle against the Syrian regime, was openly supported by the US and its Western allies including Turkey.

To a large extent ISIS was able to achieve its success in Iraq and Syria with the help of outside support, some open and other clandestine. Despite its denial, Turkey, a NATO country but symphatetic to ISIS's and al-Qaeda's Islamic cause under President Erdogen, clandestinely used their intelligence services to facilitate the transfer of fighters, weapons and equipment to the terrorists. In effect, Turkey acted as a conduit to allow Islamic recruits from around the world to enter Syria and Iraq through its porous southern border. In his rise to power to become the President of Turkey, Erdogen was known to support Islamic fundamentalist movements including the Moslem Brotherhood. His tolerance of al-Nusra Front and lack of criticism of ISIS aroused much concern in the West, particularly since Turkey is a major power in

NATO. In addition to Turkey's support, Qatar, a close ally of Turkey, and other Middle East Moslem countries were suspected of providing funds to ISIS and al-Qaeda.

The full extent of ISIS and al-Qaeda support and where it came from may never be fully revealed. However, the brand new Toyota pickup trucks with machine guns mounted on them, which the terrorists were driving, were not purchased at a local auto dealership. Given its outstanding intelligence services, the United States must have been well aware of the outside support to ISIS and al-Qaeda and where it came from, but decided to adopt a wait-and-see approach since both terrorist organizations were assisting the Free Syrian Army to defeat Assad. The ouster of Syria's Assad was considered by the United States to be the prime objective. Assad's defeat would provide the US with a friendly country on the Medeterranian Sea and on Israel's border. An initial agreement between US and Turkey to use ISIS in conjunction with the Free Syrian Army to oust Assad cannot be fully discounted. Nonetheless, over time US tolerance of Turkey's use of hardline Jihadist elements as proxies in the fight to overthrow Syria's Assad began to diminish as their terrorist actions, including commitment of atrocities, began to be publicized in the world media. In time, the tide against ISIS started to turn as pressure from nations around the world, appalled by their brutality and concerned by their growing strength, began to intensify. It also prompted the US to adopt a forceful policy toward the hard-line ISIS militants and rethink its relationship with the Free Syrian Army. Providing FSA, a borderline Islamic terrorist group, with training, weapons and intelligence and their use as a proxy army against Syria's Assad was not effective, as their allegiance was foremost to the Islamic cause. At times weapons provided to FSA were transferred to ISIS. As the US started to sever its relationship with the FSA, it shifted its support to the Syrian Democratic Forces (SDF), a YPG (People's Protection Units) Kurdish faction, as a proxy army against ISIS. This did not sit well with Turkey which considers the YPG organization to be affiliated with the anti-Turkey terrorist PKK (Kurdistan

Worker's Party) group responsible for the deaths of about 40,000 of Turkish lives.

In Iraq, the most senior Shia Cleric Grand Ayatolla Ali-Sistani issued a call to arms in June 2014 as the militants widened their grip in the north and threatened to march south toward Baghdad. After intense battles, the Iraqi forces, supported by Iranian and Kurdish fighters as well as by US air strikes, pushed the ISIS terrorists north and recaptured Mosul in December 2017, marking the defeat of ISIS in Iraq.

In Syria, Russia intervened militarily in September 2015, after an official request by the Syrian government which was on the verge of being defeated by a combined assault of ISIS, al-Qaeda in Syria, the Free Syrian rebel forces and numerous other smaller Islamic groups opposed to Syria's Assad. By early 2019, Syria with the help of Russian airpower was able to regain control of most central and western parts of Syria including most of the larger cities. In eastern Syria, the combined forces of Syrian Democratic Forces (SDF), consisting mostly of Kurds, and allied US and British airpower defeated a stubborn ISIS resistance. In the middle of 2019, the United States declared that ISIS has been defeated. On October 27, 2019, ISIS leader Abu Bakr al-Baghdadi was killed in an US raid on a compound in northern Syria, only 5 miles from the border of Turkey. The human toll from the 15 years of hostilities in Iraq and Syria was enormous. Hundreds of thousand people have been killed and more than 12 million displaced. The Syrian conflict has also brought on a serious breach in relations between two NATO allies, the United States and Turkey, as differences between them developed on a number of important issues.

On July 15, 2016, an unsuccessful coup attempt carried out by a faction within the Turkish Armed Forces tried to oust the government of President Recep Erdogen. The Turkish government concluded that the coup leaders were linked to the Gulen movement which is designated as a terrorist organization by the Republic of Turkey. The movement is led by Fethullah Gulen, a Turkish businessman and cleric who lives on a vast estate in Pennsylvania, US. President Erdogen and his government intelligence organization strongly suspected, despite United States denial, that US intelligence was at least aware of the coup but did not alert Turkey. US complicity with the coup attempt was never ruled out by Turkey. After the unsuccessful coup attempt, unconfirmed reports emerged that Russian intelligence intercepted messages of an immenent coup and alerted the Turkish intelligence operatives.

As a reaction to the failed coup d'etat, the Turkish government carried out mass purges of suspected Gulen sympathizers and demanded that the US extradite Gulen to Turkey, which was refused by the United States. Since the attempted coup, relations between US and Turkey deteriorated rapidly and relations with Russia improved considerably.

In 2017, Turkey declared it would buy Russia's S-400 missile defence system because the United States refused to sell it an American Patriot System alternative. Turkey's decision called into question the decades-long strategic relationship between the two nations, and even Turkey's credentials to be a NATO member. It also nullified a contract for Turkey to buy US F-35 combat aircrafts, planes the S-400 is designed to shoot down. The S-400 deal further solidified a deepening relationship between Turkey's President Erdogen and his Russian counterpart Putin.

Another major disagreement between Turkey and the United States involved the relationship of US with the Syrian Democratic Force (SDF). In October 2015, when the Islamic State was making large territorial gains in Syria, the US provided the SDF with weapons and essentially used them as a proxy force against ISIS. The Turkish government strongly objected to US support of the SDF as they consider them to be part of the PKK terrorist organization which for decades has waged an insurgency in Turkey in the name of Kurdish independence. Since 2016, Turkey has launched three anti-SDF operations across its border to prevent the formation of a Kurdish corridor in northern Syria: Euphrates Shield (2016), Olive Branch (2018) and Peace Spring (2019).

EVIL TWO - IRAN

Relations between US and Iran have consistently been hostile since a group of Iranian revolutionaries took 52 Americans hostage at the American Embassy in Tehran in November 1979. Following the overthrow of the Shah of Iran in the same year, Iran became strongly opposed to American presence and influence in the Middle East mainly because it curtailed their ability to dominate and control the region. Ali Khamenei, Iran's all powerful head of state and religious leader since 1989, considers the US to be an enemy of Iran and the main cause of instability of the Middle East.

On the other hand, the United States views Iran as its

main obstacle to its ability to manage the Middle East region favorably to its foreign policy goals. Specifically, Iran's master-plan is designed to penetrate diplomatically, economically and militarily the governments of some of its neighboring states, including Iraq, Syria, Lebanon, and Yemen, to establish a path of dominance in the region extending from Tehran to Beirut. If successful, Iran would pose a threat to US allies in the region, particularly Israel and Saudi Arabia.

The US also strongly opposes Iran's nuclear and ballistic missile programs which could change the balance of power in the Middle East. Equally important, Iran forms a roadblock to US extension of its influence northward towards Russia and eastward across Afghanistan towards China, countries it considers to be its long term threats.

Considering a direct military conflict with Iran as too risky and costly, the US and some of its European allies resorted to mainly economic sanctions on Iran with the intent to compel it to alter its aggressive policies.

With respect to the Iranian nuclear program, an agreement

was reached in Vienna on July 14, 2015, between Iran and P5+1 (the five permanent members of the United Nations Security Council - China, France, Russia, United Kingdom, United States - plus Germany), to significantly limit Iran's nuclear program. The agreement, called the Joint Comprehensive Plan of Action (JCPOA), lifted UN, EU and US sanctions on Iran in exchange for intrusive inspections of Iran's nuclear sites and significant limitations on Iran's nuclear technology for 10 to 15 years. Three years later on May 18, 2018, the United States under the Trump administration terminated its participation in the JCPOA citing that it failed to protect America's national security interests and reimposed sanctions on Iran, resulting in a sharp downturn in its economy. As a result, America's relationship with its European allies who continue to adhere to the pact has been damaged.

On January 4, 2020, a US missile strike near Baghdad International Airport killed Lt General Qassem Soleimani, the Iranian leader of the foreign wing of Iran's Revolutionary Guard, and the second-in-command of Iraq's Popular

Mobilization Units (PMU), Abu Mahdi al-Muhandis. Soleimani was considered the second most important Iranian leader next to Khamenei. Responding to Soleimani's assassination, Iran fired 15 ballistic missiles on Iraq's bases housing US forces. There were no US troop casualties as Iran's intention to strike the bases were conveyed to the US via the Iraqi government. The warning enabled the US to take precautionary measures. It is likely that Iran's intention was to demonstrate its capability, without inflicting heavy casualties which could have ignited a military conflict between them. However, in the aftermath of the assassination of Iran's Soleimani the Iraqi parliament passed a non-binding resolution to end the presence of foreign troops in Iraq. US response to the resolution was negative, but the training of Iraqi troops has diminished and the US troops are essentially bunkered down on the bases. In addition, the hostile relations between the United States and Iran have increased markedly and are unlikely to improve in the near future as Iran tries to increase its political and military influence in Iraq, Syria and Lebanon to the detriment of the US position in the region. Barring an accidental, unintended development of full hostilities between Iran and the United States, the tense confrontations will continue for the foreseeable future. The aftermath of a full scale war between the two adversaries would only involve the US in a quagmire similar to Afghanistan.

EVIL THREE - NORTH KOREA

North Korea has to a great extent complicated the United States political and military position in Asia-Pacific.

The political and diplomatic relations between North Korea and the United States have been historically hostile going back to the Korean War between June 1950 and July 1953. North Korea, supplied and advised by the Soviet Union, invaded the South on June 25, 1950. The United Nations, with the United States as the principal participant, entered the war on the side of the South Koreans, and the People's Republic of China came to North Korea's aid.

Over 30,000 US soldiers were killed during the war before

the Korean Armistice Agreement ended hostilities. The agreement created the Korean Demilitarized Zone (DMZ) to separate North and South Korea and allowed for the return of prisoners. No peace treaty was ever signed, and the two Koreas are technically still at war.

In recent years relations between the US and North Korea have been particularly aggravated by North Korea's nuclear and ballistic missile programs. Specifically, North Korea's multiple tests of nuclear weapons and long-range missiles capable of striking targets thousand of miles away pose a significant threat to the United States and its allies South Korea and Japan.

In addition, North Korea has on several occasions threatened to strike the United States and South Korea. In reply to the threats, US imposed sanctions on North Korea. Recently North Korea and United States have started some formal diplomacy after the first Trump-Kim summit in 2018. However, several talks between US and North Korea on denuclearizing the Korean peninsula have yielded little progress. The main issue is the distrust between the US and the North Korean leader King Jong-un to adhere to any agreement reached. If North Korea gives up the nuclear weapons, its ability to defend itself against a future military operation by the US would be severely curtailed. North Korea would almost entirely have to depend on China for its protection. North Korea's friendly overtures to South Korea have to some extent irritated the US government, since they see them as not being genuine. All indications point to a frozen state in US and North Korea relations for the foreseeable future, and North Korea's threat to US forces in the region and its allies South Korea and Japan will continue.

SOME 20 YEARS LATER

Looking back at the State of the Union address of January 29, 2002, in which President George Bush singled out Iraq, Iran and North Korea as the Axis of Evil that needed to be confronted by the United States, not much has changed to lessen the threat from these countries.

On January 8, 2020, 18 years later, 5000 US soldiers sought safety in bunkers on an Iraqi military base as Iran's Islamic Revolutionary Guard Corps (IRGC) launched numerous ballistic missiles at the Ayn al-Asad airbase in western Iraq in retaliation for the killing of Iran's General Soleimani by the US. Frustration had set in as the US had difficulty to brake Iraq away from Iran's influence. The killing of General Soleimani demonstrated this frustration, and raised the question of whether it violated Iraq's sovereignty and some aspects of international law. The next day, on January 9, 2020, the Iraqi Parliament, in response to the killing of Soleimani, passed a resolution to end the presence of foreign troops in Iraq. Conversely, Iran's position in the Middle East has strengthened by its ability to infiltrate Syria, Iraq and Lebanon both politically and militarily. Iran's response to the killing of its general was modest, but it demonstrated its capability to inflict significant damage to US forces in a future confrontation with the United States.

In Asia, North Korea has shown the ability to withstand the US demand to change course and abandon its nuclear and ballistic missile programs. Its nuclear warhead stockpile is estimated at 35 warheads, and growing. North Korea's relations with South Korea have moderated somewhat as both countries try to find some common ground for peaceful coexistence leading to a possible reunification in distant future.

Some of the joint US and South Korea military exercises have been curtailed in scope to appease North Korea.

The United States preoccupation with Iraq, Iran and North Korea for the past 20 years allowed the major US threat countries, Russia and China, time to strengthen their positions in the world. Equally important, some of the US foreign policy initiatives related to the Middle East and the world in general led to disagreements with its EU and NATO allies, as their geopolitical objectives began to differ. The political and military support the US received in the past from its main West European allies, France, Germany and Italy, to confront hostile dictatorships has waned over time, as nation building and meddling with dictatorships in the Middle East became a lower priority for them. Support was often not at the level that the US would have liked. Their main focus became to build a more effective European Union as differences among its members started to emerge, with some nations contemplating to join Great Britain in leaving the Union. In the long term the EU would like to establish its own defense capability which contradicts the US position as it prefers the Western Nations to look at NATO as their prime defense. The US involvement in the Middle East has also affected its relationship with Turkey, an important NATO member with the second largest armed forces behind the United States and a major regional power. Turkey's support of Jihadist militants, its opposition to the Kurdish dominated Syria Democratic Force (SDF), and its acquisition of Russian S-400 anti-aircraft missile defense system caused major policy disagreements between them. On the other hand, Turkey's relationship with Russia has solidified and there have been frequent consultations and meetings between Presidents Erdogen and Putin. On a number of occasions, when there were policy disagreements with the United States, Turkey threatened to close access to the Incirlik Airbase for US forces where an arsenal of a large number of nuclear bombs is stored.

Even though the overthrow of Saddam Hussein was considered at the time to be an important victory and a major step forward to extend US influence in the Middle East, in the long run it proved to be a very costly undertaking with significant losses in US lives and dollars, without any progress in solidifying the US position in the region. The events that followed engulfed the whole Middle East in turmoil, at the end of which it left the US in a position to consider a retreat from the area.

The large undertaking to reform the nations of the region to western style democracies failed mainly because it infringed on their centuries-long traditional ways of life and their sovereignties. There always was a strong resentment by the peoples of the Middle East to the presence of foreign troops on their lands.

Today, the US position in the world is very different than it was two decades ago when it emerged victorious from the Cold War seemingly poised to assume an unchallenged leadership of the world. Some former steadfast allies are confused about US foreign policy and others openly question it. Some explore more predictable partners elsewhere. The US goal to export liberal democracy to the Middle East and other parts of the world, as a step toward a new world order under the authority of the United States, is not realistic anymore, as Russia and China are rapidly emerging as equals.

CURRENT STATE OF THE WORLD

The changing balance of power is making it increasingly clear that the US is destined to share some of its world status with both Russia and China. Still other nations are likely to join them in the next decades, creating a multipolar world in the future.

China is rapidly advancing both economically and militarily to superpower status and is poised to challenge the United States in the near future. Russia is a superior military power. However, it does not posses the economic strength of either US or China. Excluding the economic aspect, there are in 2020 fundamentally three superior powers in the world, the United States, Russia and China. All three nations possess the conventional and nuclear weapons to fully challenge each other in a potential conflict. In an unlikely full scale conventional warfare encounter, the losing side could conceivably turn to a nuclear attack as a last resort.

The overall balance of military power between them favors the United States and Russia. However, the margin is narrowing and relatively insignificant as all three nations have acquired the capability to virtually destroy each other with nuclear weapons. The exact number of nuclear warheads each country possesses is a closely held national secret. Best estimates of total nuclear warhead inventory for both US and Russia are about 6000 warheads, with 1600 each deployed strategically. China's stockpile is about 400 warheads.

In an all-out nuclear war the size and capabilities of a country's conventional armed forces are relatively insignificant. It's the nuclear-tipped missiles fired from a variety of platforms that deliver the deadly punch. Hypersonic missiles that travel at more than five times the speed of sound (over

5000 miles per hour) and deployed in waves of swarms are under development. These sophisticated weapons, controlled by artificial intelligence designed to avoid interception and capable of catastrophic destruction, will negate a full preemptive attack by any of the three military powers against each other to gain unilateral superiority. No full proof defense against such an attack exists now and is unlikely to be developed in the near future. Only a madman at the helm of one of the three nations would attempt an all-out nuclear war against the others.

To avoid a conflict that could result in deployment of world destructive nuclear weapons prompts the United States, Russia and China to employ full spectrum asymmetric warfare, in which unconventional methods are merged and synchronized to provide an effective attack on its adversary. Some tactics may simply involve media misinformation, false accusations, propaganda, support of protest movements and expulsion of diplomatic personnel. More sinister tactics could involve interference in political processes, cyber attacks, economic subversion, sanctions, use of paramilitary forces and proxies, threats of conventional or nuclear attacks, chemical and biological warfare attacks, direct energy attacks, espionage, poisonings and even assassinations. On the military side, the adversary could be intimidated by land or sea military exercises, near-border airborne operations and off-shore patrols by difficult to detect submarines equipped with nuclear missiles.

These unconventional confrontations between United States, Russia and China are tantamount to a series of chess games. Some chess pieces may be taken off the board by each side as the games progress, but there will be no checkmate, as the risk of attempting a full military victory is too high.

To a large extent the balance in military power between US, Russia and China also prevents them from engaging militarily against lesser, but problematic, opponents who challenge them in crucial regions of the world. A prolonged engagement with a formidable opponent could result in major destruction of its military assets and high casualties, which would greatly benefit their main adversaries. Beyond doubt, the restraint shown by the United States from attacking Iran or North Korea (2nd or 3rd nations of evil), Russia to fully occupy Ukraine and China to retake Taiwan can largely be attributed to the existing balance of power.

While the great power stalemate continues for the foreseeable future, regional conflicts and internal discords, given the increasingly disordered global environment, are likely to accelerate. The most probable areas of conflict will be the Middle East, Asia, North Africa and Eastern Europe.

In 2020, the world was seriously afflicted by an infectious disease called COVID-19. It was first identified in December 2019 in Wuhan, China and has resulted in an ongoing deadly pandemic throughout the world. Millions of infections and fatalities have occurred. In addition, the pandemic has severely affected the economies of the world. The origin of the pandemic remains a mystery. A preliminary World Health Organization (WHO) report by a 12-nation team of scientists did not provide a firm conclusion as to the origin of COVID-19. Biological warfare has never been fully ruled out by WHO. The uncertainties related to the outbreak of the pandemic and the inability to fully control its spread has made the world a more confused, anxious and unpredictable place.

UNITED STATES IN 2020

US relations with its main rivals, Russia and China, have at times been adverse, nevertheless, open hostilities were avoided. Russia represents a mostly military threat, while China's threat is both military and economic. In both cases prospects for improving relations are not favorable, since gaining influence in Russia's and China's backyards is the main thrust of US foreign policy.

On November 3, 2020, the United States elected Joseph Biden, the former Vice President in President Obama's administration, as the 46th President of the US, despite President Trump's allegations of election improprieties.

Donald Trump's erratic presidency ended, but America's systemic challenges remain.

Domestically, economic inequality and racial bias persist in the country. The healthcare system is inadequate to meet the needs of American people, which became abundantly clear with the advance of the COVID-19 pandemic. Initially hospital facilities were inadequate to handle the large influx of patients and there was lack of life-saving equipment. A biased media violates the basic press code of fair and impartial reporting. Social media giants exercise excessive influence over the American public and large corporations have too much control over government.

The leadership of the United States is divided and seems powerless to resolve the nation's pressing problems in a bipartisan manner. During President Trump's administration the policy disagreements and lack of mutual cooperation between the Republican President and the Democratic side of the legislature reached unprecedented levels, preventing the adoption of any meaningful legislation. Democratic Party attempts to impeach President Trump in 2019 and 2020 failed when Senate Republicans voted against it.

America's strength lies in its technology base and highly skilled people who work at an extreme pace to continually develop technological innovations. Some of the products they develop and produce have no equal in the world. This technological prowess gives the United States a formidable economic and military edge.

On account of its technological strength, the United States has become a wealthy country with a relatively high standard of living enjoyed by many Americans, even when compared to some of the wealthier West European countries like Germany and France. Nevertheless, most of the wealth is concentrated in a relatively small percentage of the US population, the American elite. This economic inequality has gained ground over the years and is now affecting an increased segment of the US population. For the American middle class wages are not keeping pace with the rising cost of living. Their education places them in the cultural middle class, but their wages have moved them closer to the poverty line as debt keeps accumulating. Ten percent of the US population, is below the poverty line, with Black Americans having by far the highest poverty rate, as America is becoming increasingly segregated by wealth and race.

Over the past 70 years, White Americans in great numbers moved to suburbs surrounding large cities and smaller towns, as Americans of other races moved into cities seeking jobs and better opportunities. This trend is fully demonstrated by demographics of large US cities over the years. In 1950, shortly after the end of World War II, the population of New York City was roughly 90 percent White (incl. Hispanic White), 9.5 percent Black and .5 percent Asian plus others. In 2020, the statistics are 42 percent White (incl. Hispanic White), 26 percent Black and 32 percent Asian plus others. But these statistics do not fully demonstrate the demographic differences in large American cities since the wealthier, mostly White population, is usually concentrated in small pockets of the cities, whereas the percentage of non-White, poorer population, is even greater in the remaining disadvantaged areas or ghettos of the city. In 2020, the wealthy New York City Upper East Side District is 75 percent White and only 3 percent Black. The demographic statistics are similar in other large American cities, severely testing the premise that the fabled melting pot of this country is the source of America's strength and vigorousness by transforming people of every color and background into "One America".

Melting pots are created when businesses search for cheaper labor to increase profits or lower the cost of their products. In the South, Black slaves were imported to work the cotton fields, Mexicans came to provide cheap labor on Western farms and immigrants from around the world came to work in Midwestern industrial plants and coal mines at lower wages than the native counterparts. To harmonize people of different nationalities, religions and races takes time. People of different nationalities blend into American mainstream in a generation or two. People of different religions, like Moslems, take longer. To overcome race differences is most difficult and can take centuries. America today is not there yet. In the long run, America's racial divide could weaken its ability to function as a united nation.

On January 6, 2021, a large group of President Trump's radical rightwing supporters stormed the United States Capitol in an attempt to prevent the formalization of President-elect Joe Biden's election victory and overturn his defeat in the 2020 presidential election. Breaching police perimeters, rioters than occupied, vandalized and ransacked parts of the building for several hours. Some of the rioters were White male supremacists, who came out of the closet to show that they are still relevant, but the majority of others who joined them were ordinary citizens who wanted to show their displeasure at the current state of affairs in America. The insurrection led to the evacuation and lockdown of the Capitol building as well as six deaths. Eventually order was restored, but the event clearly demonstrated a widespread disillusion with the US democratic system. The idea of liberal democracy being a cure-all was tested as never before. It showed that democracy is difficult to sustain if its just a slogan used repeatedly by politicians and administration officials to appease a discontented citizenry. Democracy can only be truly functional as a socio-economic system when it equally supports all citizens that strive to maintain it. Unfortunately, in the real world perfect democracy doesn't exist. Some in the crowd were vandals, but the majority of the protesters wanted to demonstrate for change so they too can share the wealth of the country. In today's America, the resentment expressed by these less privileged Whites is complimented by resentment building up as well among minorities who allege that "Black Lives Matter".

In 2020, the image of the United States as a powerful nation shaping the future of the world diminished to a great extent. Trump's refusal to acknowledge his election defeat and his claim of election fraud, a pretense often associated with despotic dictatorships in lesser developed countries, and the storming of the Capitol building by a right-wing pro-Trump mob gave the US a "black eye" in the minds of the world.

America's geopolitical standing was already weakened by Russia's resurgence under Putin, China's ascending position in Asia and its inability to shape a peaceful pro-US Middle East.

US relations with the European Union have diverged to some extent as Washington insists on greater contribution to NATO by EU member states. The EU, however, would like to develop its own defense capability which would allow it to have a more independent foreign policy. Currently, EU foreign affairs are mostly dictated by NATO under US control. The close transatlantic relationship that existed between US and Europe during the Cold War has diminished over time as the European Union seeks a more collaborative policy between them, devoid from political pressure and guidance.

When Donald Trump took over the Presidency of the United States from Barak Obama on January 20, 2017, the defeat of ISIS was the main thrust of US military and foreign policy. The expectation was that when ISIS is defeated, the Middle East will become more manageable. This did not turn out to be the case. ISIS was declared defeated in the middle of 2019, nonetheless, the chaos in the region continues as numerous parties, each with its own agenda, attempt to gain advantage.

For many years the policy proclaimed some 30 years ago was accepted by US allies in Western Europe and Asia-Pacific as a common endeavor to provide lasting security in the world. However, starting with invasion of Iraq in 1993, the US directed policy only created turmoil, devastation and uncertainty where it was applied. Democracy never prevailed and corruption became widespread. In the Middle East, the policy created deeper divisions among the region's nations and brought on the proliferation of terrorism. People from the affected Middle East countries fled the destruction, famine and death that the conflicts created. Many tried to find their way to European countries to start a new life. Their reception was not always friendly. With the migratory contributions, by the year 2030, about half of the European countries will have a 10 percent or higher Moslem population. Brussels, home of the European Union headquarters, already has a 25 percent Moslem population. Most of the Moslem refugees will become good citizens of their new countries, but there could also be dangerous former members of ISIS among them.

The unsettled environment created by the Middle East conflicts has undermined the established national order, which allowed Turkey and Iran to increase their influence in the region and chart their own course to the detriment of the US policy. Turkey, an important NATO member, has embarked on an independent course to eradicate its Kurdish threat and strengthen its branch of Moslem order in the region. Its close collaboration with Russia and Iran increasingly creates disorder and confusion within NATO and threatens its effectiveness. In the long run, the combined actions of Russia, Turkey and Iran will either force the US out of Iraq and Syria, or severely limit its ability to influence the events of the region. In recent months, the heavily fortified Green Zone in Baghdad, home to the US embassy, and Iraqi air bases hosting US soldiers have been targets of repeated rocket attacks by Iraqi pro-Iranian groups. There have been calls from these groups for the US to exit Iraq or face more attacks to be forced out. The United States has stated that it is committed to withdrawing combat forces from Iraq, but didn't set a timeline. Increasingly, some West European and Middle Eastern allies have begun to question the effectiveness of the United States policy in the region. In fact, the Middle East has become a quagmire for the United States from which it has difficulty to extract itself.

After more than 20 years of US involvement in the Afghanistan war, the United States is planning to withdraw all its forces from the country on September 2021. The withdrawal comes with major risks as the Taliban could expand its control over Afghanistan, and the ongoing peace process between the group and the Afghan government could collapse.

Despite some of its recent domestic and international setbacks, the United States remains a powerful nation with extensive influence on world affairs. In the coming years

Russia's resurgence and China's economic as well as military advances will compel the US to move the major thrust of its foreign policy to the East. Facing two formidable opponents in Russia and China may prove to be very challenging for the United States.

RUSSIA IN 2020

After the dissolution of the Soviet Union in 1991, it took Russia 30 years to reestablish itself as a world military power and become a significant shaper of world events. Much of the credit for its revival has to be attributed to Vladimir Putin, a shrewd and forceful autocratic leader who continues to serve as President of Russia since 1999. Putin considers the break-up of the Soviet Union as the greatest tragedy in Russia's history. His attempts to regain some control over the lost republics run counter to US policy to promote democratic and Western oriented governments in these nations, and in this way reduce Russia's influence over them.

Russia's strategy in foreign, security and defense policies is designed to restore Russia's great power status and at the same time control its backyard of former republics to prevent them from leaving Russia's orbit. While Russia's actions may have defensive origins, they are at times carried out in an aggressive manner and infringe on the sovereignty of its neighbor states.

In February 2014, Victor Yanukovych, the pro-Russian President of Ukraine, was removed from office by West-leaning Ukrainian nationalists supported by the US and its European allies. To counter the loss of a Russia-friendly former Soviet Republic, Putin annexed Crimea and entrenched Russia-supported separatists in the Donetsk and Luhanks Republics of eastern Ukraine. Although a Minsk ceasefire agreement was concluded between the warring parties, sporadic hostilities continue and have become a major source of disagreement between Russia and the West, resulting in Russia's suspension from the Group of Eight (G-8) inter-governmental political forum. Resolution of the conflict is difficult since the Russia-backed separatists seek a special status in the Ukrainian Government, which is unacceptable to Western oriented Ukrainian nationalists.

The return of Crimea to Ukraine is a non-issue for Russia. Crimea has a majority Russian speaking population and contains a large naval base vital to Russia's national security as it supports its naval operations in the Black Sea and the Mediterranean waters, as well as provides for resupply of its naval base in Tartus, Syria.

In 2020, protests erupted in Belarus, a former Soviet Republic, against President Lukashenko centered on claims of fraudulent elections and there was also an outbreak of hostilities between two former Soviet Republics, Armenia and Azerbaijan, about a disputed territory. These events in Ukraine, Belarus and Armenia indicate that Russia's backyard is getting restless.

Russia's economy is fairly stable although only middle sized at about one tenth of that of US or China. The living standard of most Russians has improved in recent years, nevertheless, it is still significantly lower than that of the

world's bigger Western economies. Direct comparison
with the West is difficult as the cost of living in Russia is
considerably lower. Russia is careful to preserve economic
stability, keeping in mind the economic collapse that led to
the dissolution of the Soviet Union. Relatively high levels of
international reserves and low external debt help Russia limit
its exposure to external pressures.

Despite some domestic issues, including wealth inequality
and corruption, Putin gets a relatively high rating from the
Russian people mainly because they appreciate and support
his efforts to put Russia on the world center stage again.
Russia's ethnicity is over 80 percent Russian and the Russian
people are highly patriotic. They love their land and often
refer to Russia as their Motherland. They showed their
courage during the siege of Stalingrad by Nazi Germany
during world War II and they would do it again if Russia was
threatened. Russia's people believe that because of its sheer
size, nuclear power and historic accomplishments it has the
right to be recognized as a great power on equal footing with

the United States and China. They don't consider that the level of economy should be a major indication of a country's strength.

Russia's military has shown a remarkable improvement and capability since the chaos that followed the dissolution of the Soviet Union. Its military support to Syria to contain the opposition forces was partially successful as it prevented the overthrow of the Assad regime. However, it failed to achieve a total defeat of the opposition or gain full control of Syria, which only indicates that in a disordered environment military power has its limits. Its interference in Syria to prevent the collapse of the Assad regime was to a great extent motivated by the necessity to confront the Islamic militants, many of whom came from the former southern Soviet Republics. If successful in Syria, the militants could then return to Russia's backyard and confront Russia itself.

The conflict in Syria has created an unexpected accommodation between Russia and Turkey, an important member of NATO. Despite a number of geopolitical disagreements, the two countries have shown the ability, to the dismay of the United States, to cooperate in other areas important to them.

Russia, specifically Putin, prefers not to ally with any country that considers itself to be in a superior position, whether its economic or military. He would only agree to an alliance if Russia is treated as an equal. His thinking is: "Russia is the largest country in the world, its history goes back 2000 years, we have weapons that can destroy the world. Why should we humble ourselves before anyone?". Russia under Putin prefers to have a free hand to move East or West, whichever is better for Russia.

After the dissolution of the Soviet Union, Russia's relations with China became progressively friendlier. In 1996, the relation progressed toward a strategic partnership and in 2001 they signed a treaty of friendship and cooperation. The two countries enjoy close relations militarily, economically and politically, while supporting each other on various global political issues before the United Nations. They never interfere publicly in each others domestic or international affairs. However, as China's ambitions and influence in Central Asia and Asia-Pacific increase, Russia is monitoring these events closely to determine if any actions taken by China are detrimental to its national interests.

Russia is fully capable of challenging the United States in both conventional and nuclear forces and as such represents a formidable threat to American interests worldwide. It is the largest and most capable rival of the United States in terms of weapons of mass destruction. Therefore, the ability of the US to bring about a change in Russia's foreign policy or its threatening posture is limited.

With the constitutional changes of 2021, Putin could be in control of Russia for the next 15 years. Given the mood in the country and his own convictions, he would never accept a submissive role for Russia. Applying too much political or military pressure on him may be very dangerous and unpredictable. Russia would prefer not to engage in direct conflict with either Western Europe or the United States.

However, it has certain red lines, especially with regard to its backyard of former Soviet Republics, that can't be crossed. Russia considers itself historically and culturally to be an European country. If given an equal world standing with the United States, it would go West. However, current US policy toward Russia pushes it to the East.

CHINA IN 2020

Despite Russia's formidable threat in Europe and Iran's inroads in the Middle East, the United States is beginning to shift its strategic center of gravity to the Asia-Pacific region as it now considers China to be its primary strategic competitor.

The People's Republic of China is a Communist State that came to power in 1949 after a long civil war with the Kuomintang led government of the Republic of China. The Communists gained control of mainland China and established the Peoples Republic of China (PRC) in 1949, forcing the leadership of the Republic of China to retreat to the island of Taiwan. PRC became a great power in 1960's and today has the world's largest population, the second largest GDP (after US) and is the world's largest manufacturer and exporter. Based on projected GDP, China will overtake the United States as the largest economy sometime before 2030. Beyond doubt, China is an emerging superpower.

In 2012, Xi Jinping became General Secretary of the Communist Party of China, a post he holds currently. China's national strategy is to return China to a position of strength, prosperity and leadership on the world stage. To advance this strategy, China has in recent years consolidated its economic growth, strengthened its armed forces and assumed an active role in world affairs.

With its "One Belt, one Road" initiative China is investing heavily in global infrastructure to secure its trade and security interests. In 2020, China concluded a Regional Cooperative Economic Partnership (RCEP) with 14 Asia-Pacific countries including Japan, South Korea and Australia. RCEP is the world's largest trade agreement in history covering a third of the world's population and valued at $26 trillion. In addition, on December 30, 2020, the EU and China concluded in principle the negotiation for a Comprehensive Agreement on Investment (CAI). The agreement will create a better balance in the EU-China trade relationship as China will commit to open up to the EU in a number of key trade sectors. On March 28, 2021, China and Iran signed a Comprehensive Strategic Partnership (CSP) agreement that will chart the two sides' economic, political and trade relations over the next 25 years.

US-China relations became particularly strained since 2017, when Washington's National Security Strategy portrayed Beijing as a major threat to American interests. The main concern of the United States is that China will replace the US as the leader of the world through its economic strength and foreign policy initiatives which infringe on traditional US allied territories including Japan, South Korea and even the European Union. China's economic and associated political expansion has the potential to replace the US as the lead country in Asia-Pacific. The region has a population of about

4 billion, a little over half of the world's, and it's still growing. Because of the area's large concentration of the world's population, it becomes a huge market for manufactured goods. In a way, the Chinese have turned the globalization concept to their own advantage by expanding interaction with a huge economic market in their own backyard without having to conform to the liberal democracy ideology, which is intended to accompany globalization.

In recent times, the political relations between Japan and China have suffered from conflict, different interpretations of history, territorial disputes and Japan's close political and defense relationship with the US. But with the opening of China to the world economy around 1990, business and economic connections between the two countries have improved substantially thanks to their geographic proximity and complementary needs. China's rising middle class provides a welcome market for a Japan mired in demographic stagnation and Japan's advanced technology offers many benefits to China. Japan's imports from China in 2020 were at about 165 billion dollars, more than twice the 70 billion dollars imports from the US.

In 2020, the United States is clearly in competition with China for world economic dominance. China's location in Asia-Pacific with more than half of world's population gives it an enormous advantage by being part of what is the world's largest market. China's large industrial capacity also allows the country to produce more goods than America.

US tensions with China in the economic arena center on large yearly trade deficits and what it considers abusive trade practices, including theft of intellectual property and transfer of technologies from US companies to their Chinese counterparts. Once China acquires advanced technologies from the West, Chinese firms then spin off these imitations and begin innovating. This practice lowers China's research and development costs.

In the political arena, the United States has issues with China's aggressive consolidation and control over contested territories in the South and East China Seas. It also condemns China's repression of Turkic Uyghur Moslems in Xinjiang, repression of Hong Kong's dissidents and aggressive intentions against Taiwan.

On the other hand, China considers that forcing other countries to accept the American democratic system only creates division, intensifies tensions and undermines stability.

A LOOK AHEAD

Despite its apparent failure in the Middle East, the US policy directive proclaimed by President George Bush in 1991 to disseminate liberal democracy and free enterprise throughout the world will continue to constitute the cornerstone of US strategy. The approach to promote the doctrine, its speed of execution and even the targeted nations may vary with Presidencies. However, the basic objective to create a secure, prosperous and democratic world under US control for the American people will remain unchanged and continue to receive full affirmation and support from the "Deep State".

With the election of Joseph Biden as the next President of

the United States in November 2020, the original policy will continue to be in full effect. However, the principal nations to be targeted will become Russia and China, as these countries are now considered the main threat to the United States. Biden had pledged to take a tougher line with Russia and China than his predecessor. In view of this, the US will likely intensify its use of full spectrum asymmetric warfare hoping that it can find a weak spot in Kremlin's and Beijing's armor, which it can exploit further. Use of sanctions will continue to be one of the primary tools to challenge Russia and China for possible indiscretions. Nonetheless, tougher actions can't be ruled out. Reciprocal actions will follow.

In the coming years the United States will find itself increasingly challenged, independently or in concert, by Russia and China. Iran and North Korea will also become significant opponents as their military capabilities increase. However, budget constraints, decades of sustained engagements in the Middle East and Afghanistan, and the inability of too many of the nation's youth to meet recruitment standards have affected its military's readiness for operations. Under these circumstances the US armed forces will be ill-equipped to handle two, near-simultaneous major regional contingencies. This predicament will have a major affect on US foreign policy decisions in the coming years.

Despite a determined effort by the United States to retain its exceptional superiority, by around 2025, it will become clear that the world has reached a multi-polar stage with the United States, Russia and China the predominant powers. The likelihood of aggressive military provocations between the three powers will diminish as their offensive capabilities reach near-parity, and any military confrontations begin to carry unacceptable high risks. Asymmetric warfare will become the main instrument of hostility. US policy emphasis will be on consolidating a coalition of its West European and Asian allies to add to the containment of Russia and China. The policy will not be universally accepted by all US allies as economic considerations will tend to prevail.

The main thrust of Russia's foreign policy will be to

undermine US alliances with Western nations including NATO and in general influence global events as a major power. Despite its large geographic size, Russia's population is relatively small at about 146 million. This makes it difficult for Russia to extend its influence world-wide, equivalent to the extent that US and China can. Russia also lacks the economic power of US or China. However, its energy supplies to Europe provide it with considerable political influence over the Continent. With the completion of the North Stream 2 pipeline in 2022, Russia will be providing Europe with about 70 percent of its natural gas needs.

In recent years Russia has built a system of defense that will make it difficult for the United States to engage in direct military confrontation without a potentially forceful retaliation. The US will be cautious to keep the pressure on Russia to a reasonable degree, as a potential military alignment with China could prove very ominous for the United States. Russia will continue to support China on most contentious international issues. But at least for now, it will avoid to get deeply involved in any major disputes between the United States and China in the Asia-Pacific region or to form a full military alliance with China.

In the near term, most of the US foreign policy focus will be on China as it becomes potentially the primary threat to the United States. For the first time in its history, the US is facing a country of comparable economic capacities and with great historic skills in conducting international affairs. This was not the case with the Soviet Union during the Cold War. In the last 20 years, China's drive to achieve its full potential went into high gear, with an important reinterpretation of the Communist ideology and wide-ranging economic changes. Through a set of sweeping reforms, China skillfully moved toward a market economy while at the same time politically retaining authoritarian rule. In a relatively short time it has overshadowed Japan and became the most influential country in Asia-Pacific. China with a population of about 4.5 times of the United States has an enormous, relatively inexpensive and well educated labor pool. Its economic growth of the past two decades will continue and propel it to the forefront of the world's economic arena. China's economic future looks very bright and it is poised to overtake the United States as the world's largest economy sometime before 2030. In addition, the Chinese Yuan is likely to join the Dollar and Euro as a world currency. This economic clout will provide China with new power and influence in Asia-Pacific. To secure its world standing China will be boosting its research into frontier technologies including semiconductors, artificial intelligence, quantum computing, biotechnology, clinical medicine and deep space, deep earth and deep sea research. The Chinese people are very proud of their accomplishments. Despite some major differences in the past, they are now on a united common mission to make China an unequal world power.

China still lags both US and Russia in military power. Nonetheless, its military rearmament is proceeding on an equal scale to its economic advances. By 2030, its navy will be competitive with that of US and Russia. Its arsenal of strategically deployed nuclear warheads will also approach those of US and Russia. China will acquire the military capabilities to match its economic prowess and in this way gain substantial influence over world affairs. However, on a number of occasions Chinese leader Xi Jinping stated that China does not seek hegemony and wants to see development of a fair global order.

Currently, China is not challenged for supremacy by any other Asia-Pacific nation. India is the only country in this region of the world that has the potential to militarily and economically stand up to China in the future. However, its development is well behind China's and its pace of development is much slower. It's highly unlikely that it would be able to mount a significant challenge to China before 2050.

The next ten years will be critical in US, China relations as diplomatic tensions between them accelerate and the fate of Taiwan is likely to come up for resolution. As with Russia, asymmetric warfare will be employed by the United States in an attempt to deter China from becoming the world's economic and military superpower. However, this approach will become problematic as the nations of Asia-Pacific aspire increasingly for peace and cooperation. Economic development is their priority.

By the end of this decade, some US progressive political leaders will urge America to end its nation building adventures, as the world becomes multipolar and dictating a certain course of conduct to other nations will not be tolerated, especially when it comes against two equally potent superpowers. They will urge for the chess games to end, as the stakes become too high for the United States, Russia and China to continue them. An accidental wrong move on the chessboard could result in a checkmate and a deadly disaster for the world.

The new policy approach will likely be opposed by the "Deep State", and a forceful debate will ensue. If the opposition is overcome, a new policy will come into effect which will emphasize US domestic well-being including a determined effort to urgently address economic inequality, racial tensions, random shootings, health care for an aging population, climate change, and the aftermath of the COVID-19 pandemic.

Plans will be developed and enacted to shore up the melting pot so it does not boil over, but accommodates all Americans regardless of race, nationality or sex. Effective education for all Americans will become a national security imperative to compete in the global knowledge-based economy. Demographic projections indicate that by 2035 older people (65+) will outnumber children (under 18) for the first time in American history. To properly take care of these older citizens a considerably expanded health care system will be enacted. America will begin to take care of democracy at home.

The United States will remain a militarily superior nation, even though it will be closely matched by Russia and China. It will continue to have the capability to defend itself against any direct aggression. To be successful, the new American leadership will have to understand that people of other nations have different genetic, cultural and moral codes developed over their centuries' long histories, which are different than theirs. In the future it will become important for America to look inward and address some key domestic issues that have been neglected for a long time.

In the next 15 years the ethnic mix of the US population will undergo some major changes as the Hispanic and Asian segments of the population grow more rapidly. Future America will have a markedly different demographic composition. The new Americans will favor a form of limited isolationism in which diplomatic, economic and cultural cooperation with other nations will be strengthened, but the military adventurism of the past will be limited. Emphasis will be on improving the lives of all Americans.

However, should the "Deep State" prevail in the debate, the old policy stays, the full spectrum asymmetric warfare remains in effect and the chess games continue. In the meantime, US, Russia and China will race to develop a new generation of powerful weapons, which will totally change the character of warfare. The survival of the world we live in and enjoy will continue to remain in jeopardy.

SOURCES

www.wikipedia.org

www.infoplease.com

www.nytimes.com

www.guardian.com

www.armscontrol.org

www.asiatimes.com

www.cnn.com

www.news.cgtn.cm

www.usatoday.com

www.forbes.com

www.thelevantnews,com

www.dw.com

www.defensenews.com

www.americanprogress.com

www.census.com

www.globalissues.com

Lightning Source UK Ltd.
Milton Keynes UK
UKHW041444200521
383961UK00018B/456/J